LIFE'S LESSONS:
A Mother's Journal

Bea Nettles

Introduction by Sandra Matthews
Preface by Terry Suhre

Inky Press Productions Urbana, Illinois

Scheduled Exhibitions of Life's Lessons: A Mother's Journal

The Chrysler Museum of Art
Norfolk, Virginia
April 21-June 24, 1990

The Illinois State Museum
Springfield, Illinois
October 27, 1991-January 19, 1992

Copyright © 1990 by Bea Nettles
All rights reserved, including the right of reproduction in whole or in part in any form.

Published by Inky Press Productions, Urbana, Illinois 61801.
Distributed by Prairie Book Arts Center, Box 725, Urbana, Illinois 61801.
Printed by Andromeda Printing, Champaign, Illinois.

Library of Congress Cataloging-in-Publication Data

Nettles, Bea, 1946-
   Life's lessons : a mother's journal / by Bea Nettles ;
  introduction by Sandra Matthews.
     p.   cm.
   ISBN 0-930810-05-8
   1. Photography, Artistic. 2. Parenting--Pictorial works.
I. Title.
TR656.N419   1990
779' .092--dc20   90-5006
                                                                                     CIP

ISBN 0-930810-05-8

*This project was supported in part by a grant from the National
Endowment for the Arts, A Federal Agency.
Additional support provided by the Illinois State Museum, Springfield, Illinois.
Thanks also to the Polaroid Corporation for their ongoing support of this work.*

Cover Design: Guido Mendez

For additional information on other titles by Bea Nettles, contact Prairie Book Arts Center, Box 725, Urbana, Illinois 61801.
Manufactured in the United States of America.

INTRODUCTION

Though it is truly gratifying to witness the beginnings of a recognition of the experiences of women, the experience of women as mothers remains largely unheard and unseen in any public forum. Mothers may talk among themselves whenever possible, but the content of these conversations is not of value in the larger society. We generally see and hear of mothers as either idealized or derogatory stereotypes, with little evidence of the complexity and potency of the experience from a mother's point of view. How is it that such a large and important group of people, whose concerns are fundamental to the survival of the species, can be culturally invisible?

According to the middle class mythology of motherhood which reached a pinnacle in the U.S. in the 1950's and still influences ideas about the family, being a mother precluded doing other kinds of work in any serious way. Procreation and creation of other kinds, reproduction and cultural production, were seen as mutually exclusive. In our present society, although many women are working mothers, a separation still exists between private and public, between the social construction of motherhood and of other kinds of work. For mothers, it is very difficult to integrate the two.

Bea Nettles' book, Life's Lesson: A Mother's Journal, tackles this difficult territory head on. She manages to connect the world of family and home with the concerns of the larger society, and to speak out about some of the difficulties of motherhood. The book functions on the interface of private and public. It is no accident that Nettles has used the journal form, a private vehicle for recording one's thoughts. Published journals have long been a channel for relocating the musings of private life in the context of a larger audience. Using the journal form, Nettles can speak in the first person, and maintain her voice and subjecthood, as a mother, consistently throughout the book.

The images in Life's Lessons are all made within the home environment, and incorporate social issues as their impact is felt at home. Home is represented both as a protected space and as a place that is completely continuous with the conflicts and threats outside. In this way, the book describes something of the pressures on the white middle class family. The idealized nuclear family...like Nettles' family, containing two children, a boy and a girl...has had to give way in recent decades to a more realistic model of the shapes families actually do take. Starting with a traditional concept of home and motherhood, then, Nettles moves out in the course of the book to show the complete intertwining of private and public concerns.

The book itself, in the way it is constructed, gives us a profound model for what could be called a maternal mode of thinking. The reader moves between polarities and layers of simultaneous experience. Through the sequencing of her images and text, Nettles oscillates between intense empathy with and more detached observation of her children, between registering their concerns and voicing her own concerns about them. For example, in the construction of many of the pictures, Nettles takes fragments of her childrens' drawings and written papers from school and recombines and interprets them. Making images out of their artifacts, she is appropriating their work and fusing it with her own in a way that merges the identities of mother and child. Yet she also introduces several layers of self-consciousness, partly through her writing and partly by often including her own image in the pictures. She talks about how her children perceive her, and watches herself watching them, critically monitoring her own role. When she places herself in the picture as an observer, she has stepped back and presented herself as a participant in the situation but with a separate identity.

This kind of shifting proximity in relation to another, balancing intimacy and individual autonomy, merging and separation, is usually seen from the child's point of view as an important part of development. Yet it is also an important part of a mother's experience. Nettles has embodied it in the structure of her book. That the experience is embodied, rather than merely referred to, is important. The implications are that the method of doing something is part of the outcome, and that important ideas are contained in experience at every level. In structure as well as in content, then, the book moves back and forth, between the literal and the metaphoric, between small personal events and larger social issues. We experience the maternal viewpoint, through Nettles' work, as full of coexisting polarities and connections between levels of experience. This seems appropriate to the task of childrearing or, for that matter, of caring for the physical and emotional needs of any human being.

In speaking about the alternation and layering of maternal experience, we cannot forget that amidst the multiple and often clamoring demands of raising children, a mother must also keep clear some very fundamental priorities, having to do with the well-being of the child. Nettles keeps this baseline very clear as well in her book, returning at the end to the themes of love, hope and the wish for strength for her children. This grounding anchors the book and serves as counterpoint to the range of ideas she otherwise engages.

We have not yet mentioned something very obvious, which is that in addition to being a mother, Bea Nettles is an artist with a public life. Most of the time this remains tacit in the book, except at the very end, when she writes, "Expressing my most urgent concerns through my work helps me to cope with the demands placed upon me." With this line, she articulates the struggle to bring together her maternal and artistic roles, to see them as vitally linked rather than mutually exclusive. Life's Lessons is a crucial contribution in the way it overcomes the unnecessary and disenabling separation of important life functions, and moves beyond what Ursula LeGuin calls "private life: a mythological space invented by the patriarchy".

Images of Nettles' hand or hands appear in various forms throughout the book. Her hands seem both to hold her children near and to hold them at a distance for scrutiny, both to caress and to restrain. Her hands slice bread and feed her children; her hands also made this book and we thank her for it.

Sandra Matthews
Associate Professor of Photography and Film
Hampshire College
Amherst, Massachusetts

PREFACE

Bea Nettles works close to the bone. Like her previous books, <u>Life's Lessons: A Mother's Journal</u> uses an autobiographical narrative that has as its source her family members, specific places and significant objects. Nettles' work is a fusion of memory, symbol, and materials through which she seeks meaning in the eternal, mother/child cycle that binds generation to generation.

In <u>Life's Lessons</u> Nettles is responding to her children's increasingly independent participation and deepening perceptions of a dangerous and wonderful world. As their horizons widen the risks increase and they become more vulnerable to influences beyond her control. Nettles documents the struggle to teach and maintain a meaningful value system that is in constant conflict with the subtly seductive messages of a materialistic, media driven society. The lessons of life take a toll spiritually as well as physically. Nettles hopes her children can "...continue to learn life's lessons and survive unbroken...". In addressing the fears, frustrations and joys of parenting, Nettles crosses the boundaries of gender, race, and generation to touch the deep, complex and most basic of all relationships...that which exists between mother and child.

Terry Suhre
Associate Curator for Art
Illinois State Museum
Springfield, Illinois
1990

Acknowledgements...
First, my most sincere thanks to my family, Lionel, Rachel and Gavin, for allowing me to create and share these images.
Linda Benedict Jones and Barbara Hitchcock of Polaroid Corporation were instrumental in supplying encouragement and all the materials, both 4x5 and 20x24, for creating these photographs. John Reuter at the Polaroid 20x24 studio helped me to restage many of the 4x5 images with great patience and a very good eye.
Brooks Johnson, Curator of Photography at the Chrysler Museum in Norfolk, Virginia was the first to present the entire body of work.
Additional thanks to Kent Smith, Director for Art, and Terry Suhre, Associate Curator for Art of the Illinois State Museum for their strong support of the exhibition and book.

Since our first child was born in 1978, I have been creating images that deal with the experience and the role of being a mother. The first evidence of this was the book Flamingo in the Dark which was a visual autobiography beginning with my childhood in Florida and ending with Rachel's first year. That book was a celebration of the life cycle, loaded with color and promise.

What followed were several years of living with very young children. I found the best way to keep working was to utilize a pinhole camera to make still lives of images Close to Home. Holidays, special clothes, nightmares, and monumental events like the birth of a baby brother were documented in this work. Days, seasons, and years passed.

As Gavin grew older and he and Rachel began to be more aware of the world outside, I incorporated their experiences and artifacts into a sequence of photo-etchings entitled Landscapes of Innocence. These stark images began to hint at the sadness and conflicts I felt as my children became aware of the darker side of life. Rachel was old enough to sense the devastating effect of her father losing his business and everything he had worked for to someone he had trusted. What followed were difficult and stressful years. Both children remember being uprooted and moved to the midwest. It is not surprising that a fear for the future began to enter my work. I began to fight off an immobilizing sense of loss.

Life's Lessons began as a set of five triptychs produced in photo-etching (Money, Luck, Hansel and Gretel, Chicken and the Egg, and Missing). Parenting keeps getting harder. The worries at home begin to compound with continued sibling rivalry, adjustment to public school, opressive materialism, gender identification, struggles with discipline and limits. In addition to this, add the very real fear of harm to one's children at the hands of strangers, concerns for their health (drugs, pollution, AIDS), and the everpresent fear of nuclear destruction.

The text within the images comes from school workbooks, classwork and notes brought home by my children. Though I place the words in a different context, none of them are fabricated.

Bea Nettles
Urbana, Illinois
1990

LIFE'S LESSONS:
A Mother's Journal

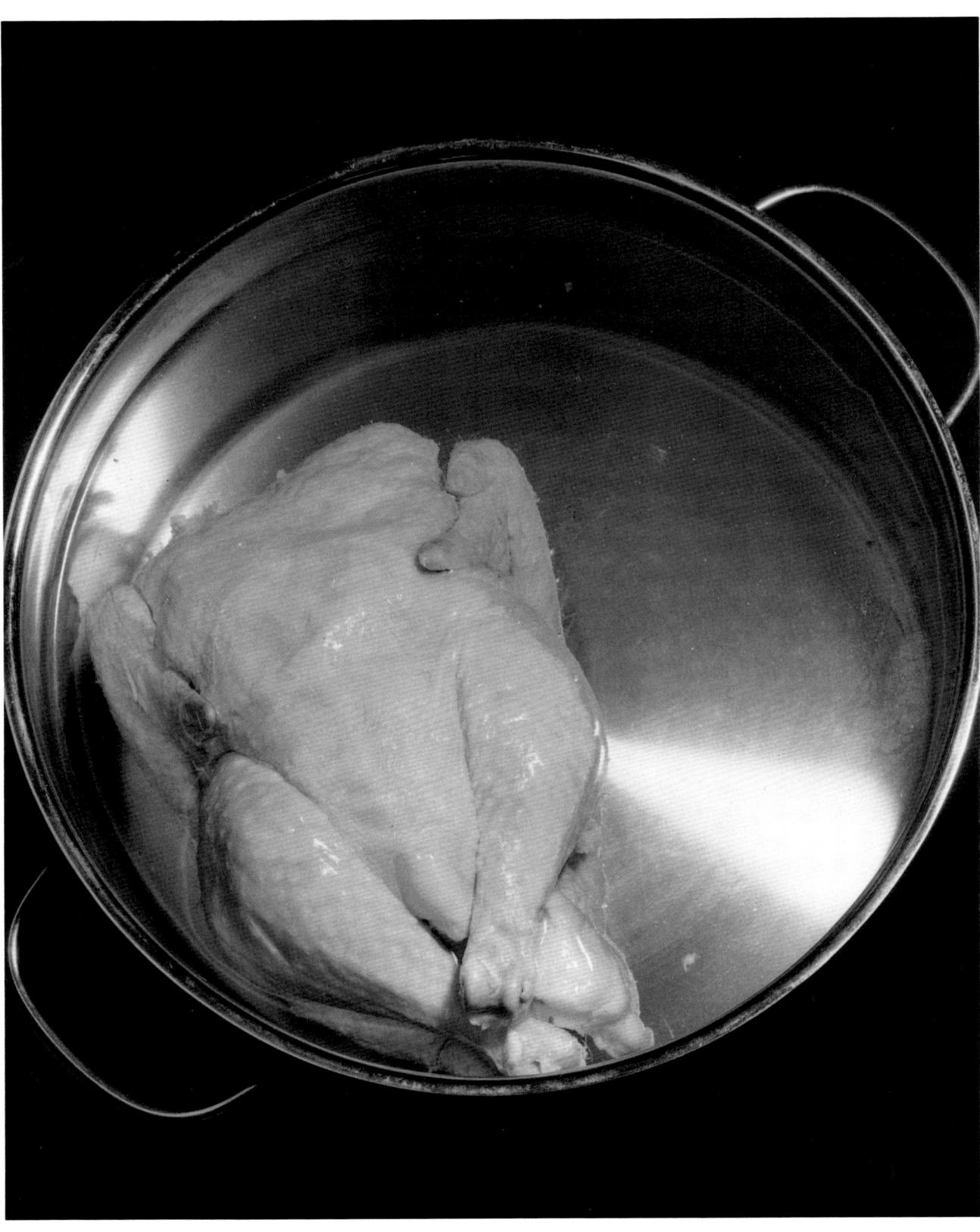

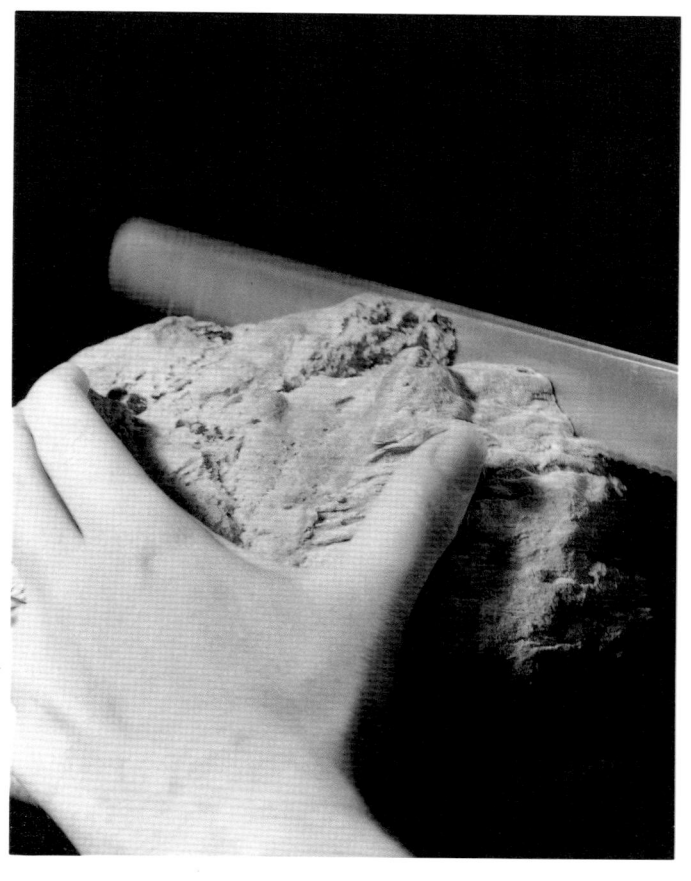

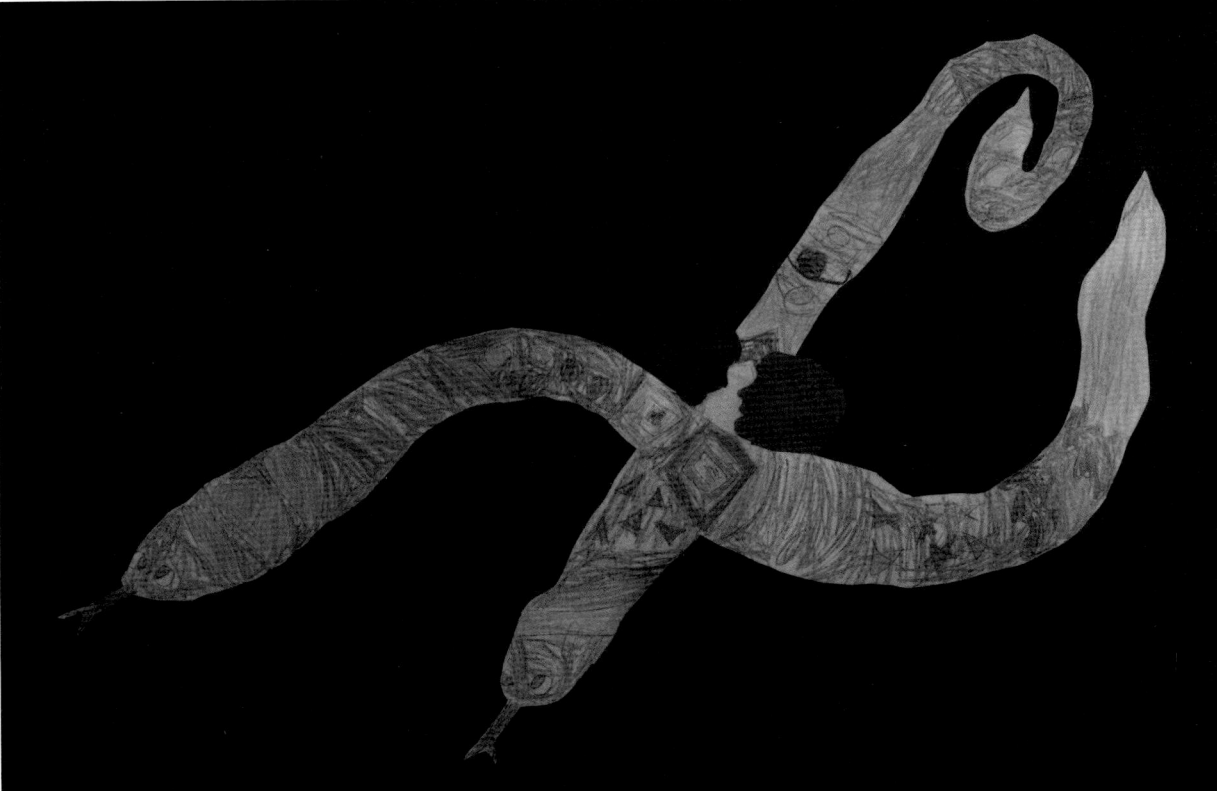

I have many <u>friends</u>,
but I have no ___.

(enemies) fun   ears

This journal begins in my home,
with images of food and bread.
As dark thoughts enter my mind like a serpent, I
think about Rachel and an entry in her school book,
"I have many friends, but I have no ____."
She first entered "fun", then changed her answer.
How sad to feel that you have no fun when you're
only eight!
I thought only grown-ups felt that way.

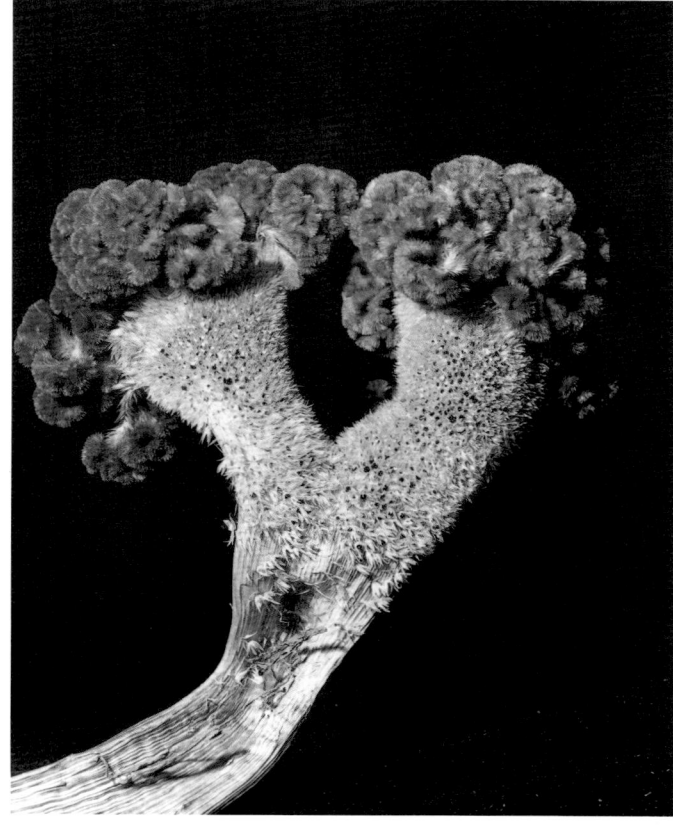

*The natural laws, such as survival of the fittest, are sometimes hard to accept....
cruel and fascinating lessons. But Nature's way is certainly preferable to the dangerous imbalance caused by humans. We're on the verge of breaking the fragile cycle and I fear for my children's future.*

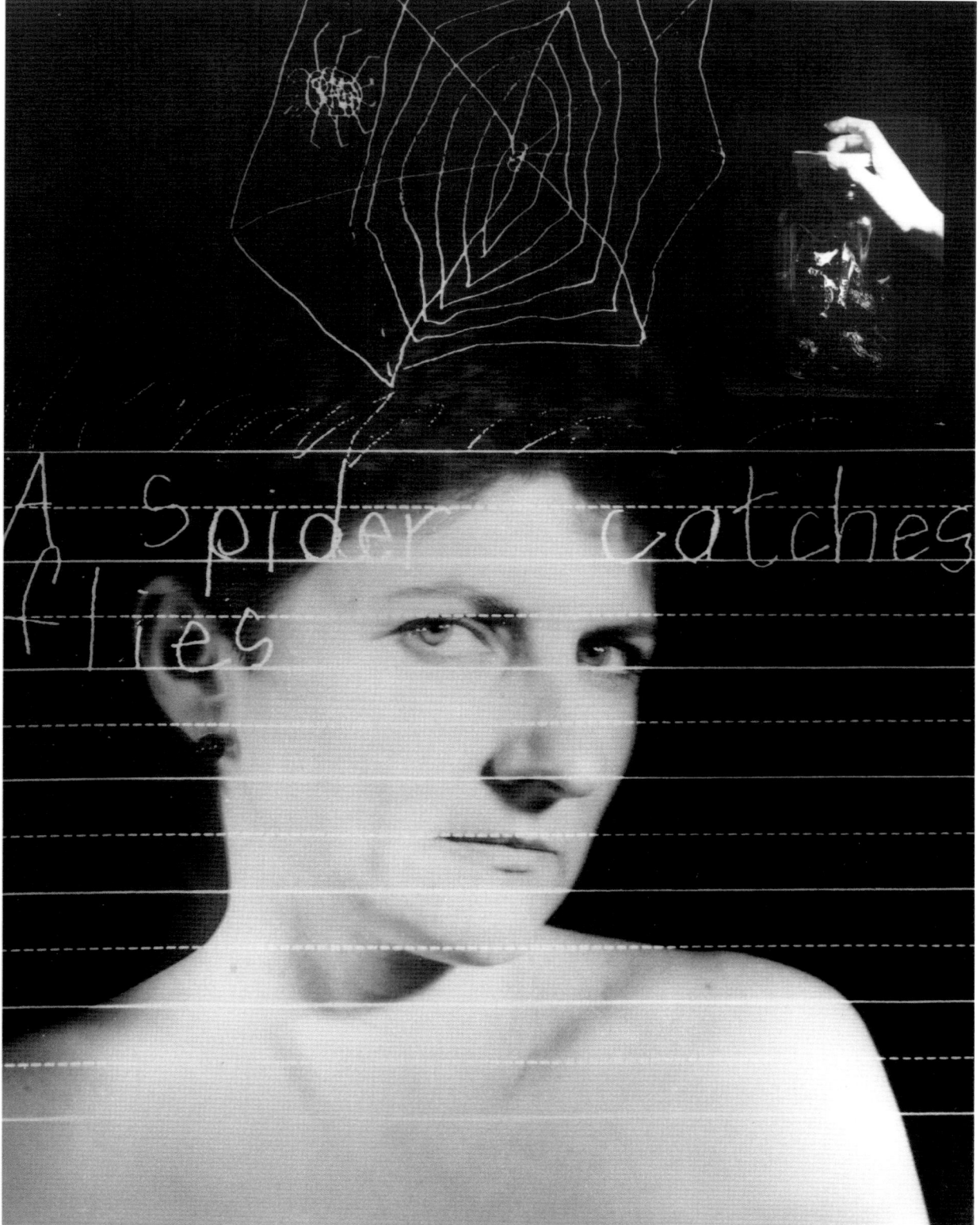

Hansel and Gretel *terrified me when I was a kid. It scared me to think that a mother could dump her kids in the woods...on purpose! Will my daughter and son know not to take the candy...not to enter the strange inviting house...not to trust the grownup (Witch)? Forced to use their own wits and good sense, will they escape unharmed?*

It is a longstanding kindergarten tradition for children to make their handprints for their moms. What's different now is that they're also being fingerprinted by the police. Fear of getting stolen is pervasive and very real, troubling discussion for the breakfast table.

When the milk carton girl was "Found", Rachel was delighted and wanted to know all the details of her homecoming. I've quit buying milk in those cartons. The endless stream of boy-girl- boy-girl was just too much.

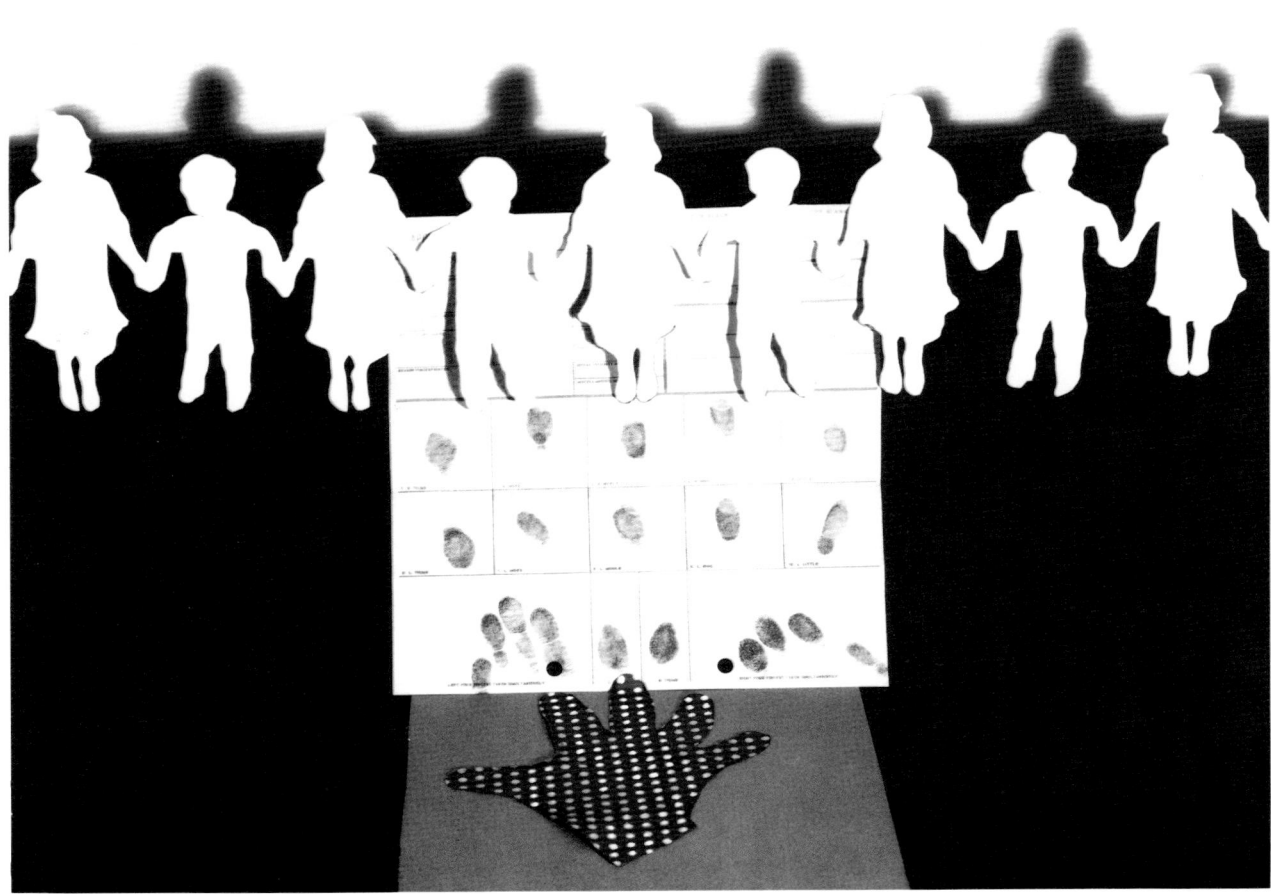

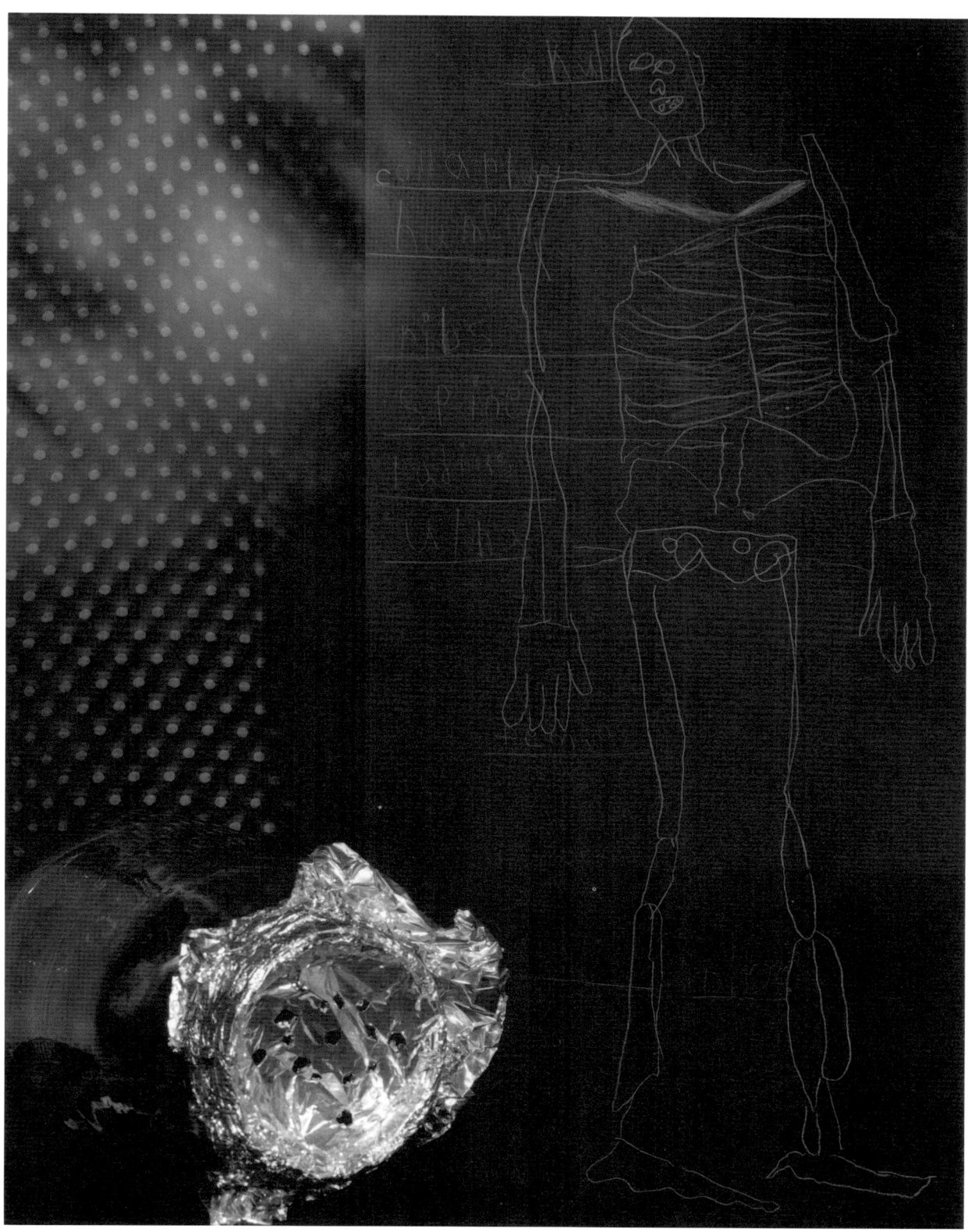

Gavin was born on a Sunday morning and we went home from the hospital the next day.

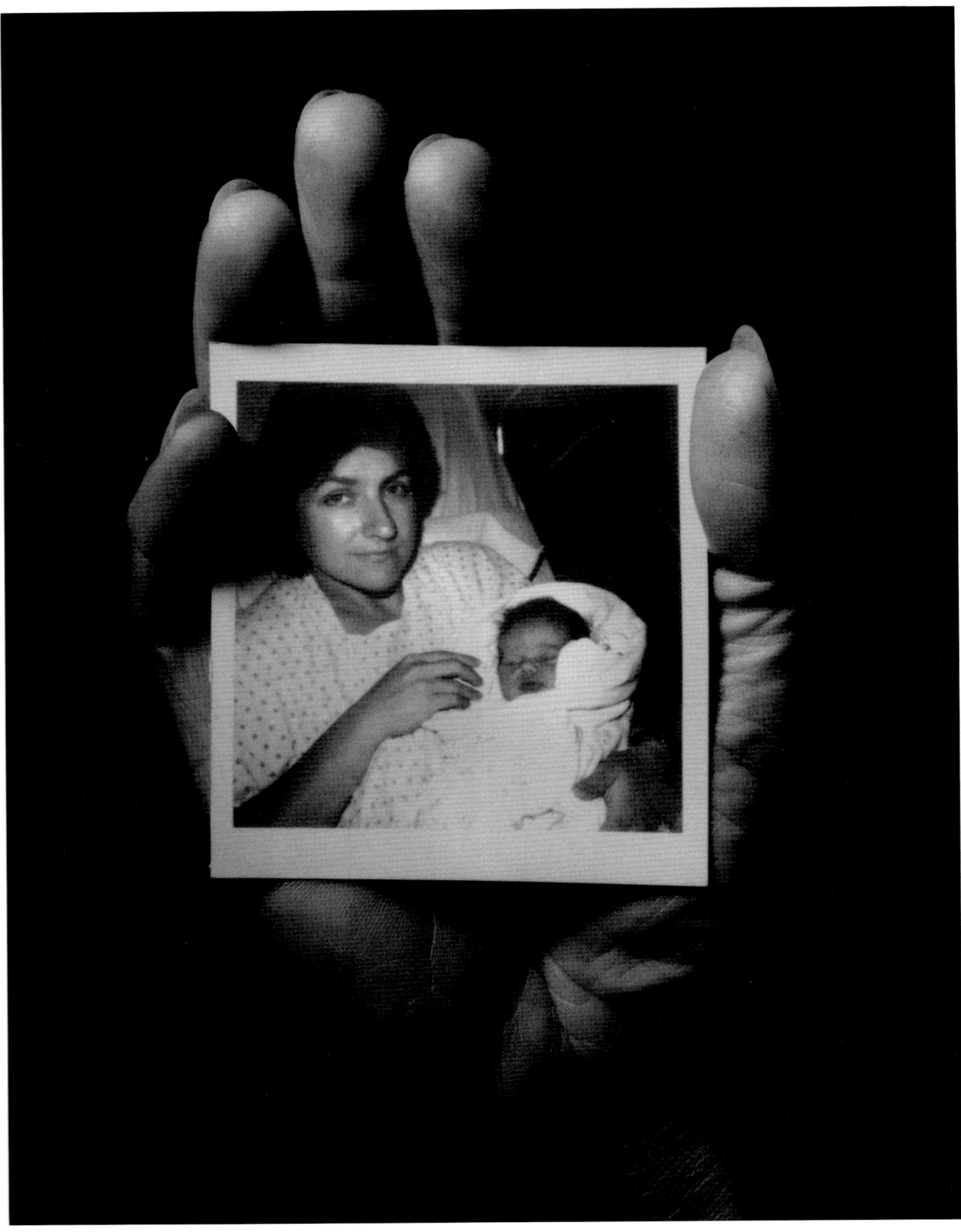

That Sunday was the only day he had me to himself. It was also the first night I'd ever spent away from Rachel. He has always had to share me, its harder for Rachel.

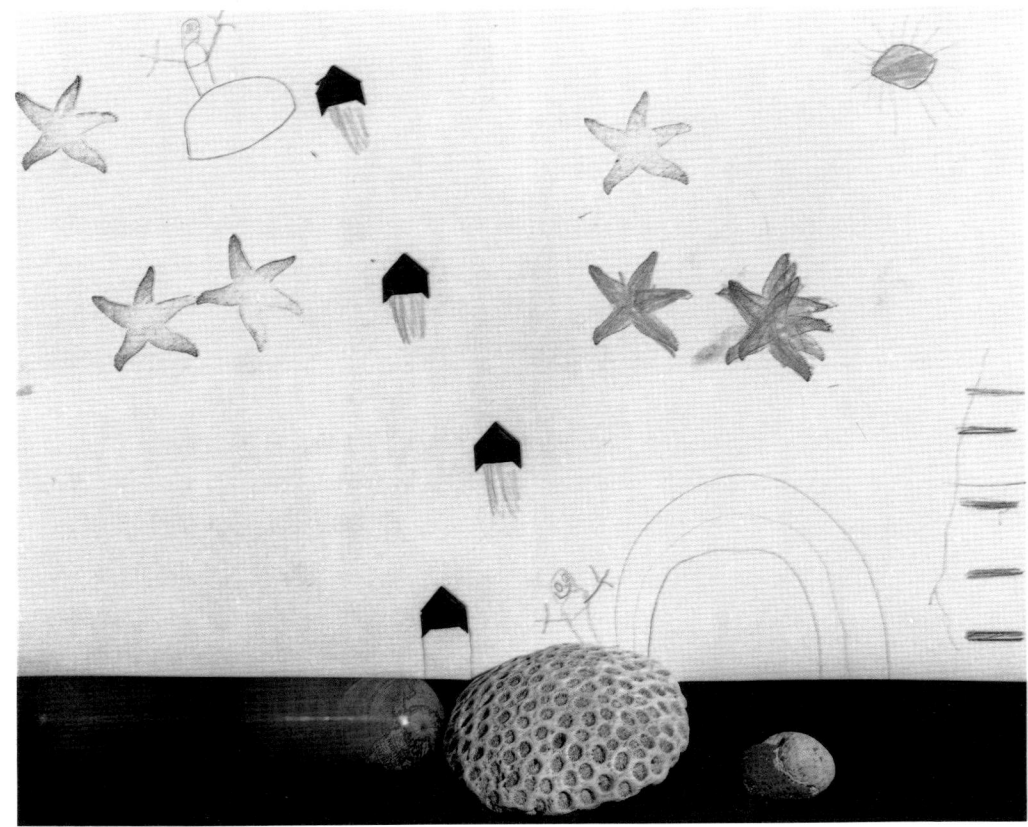

Star Wars...

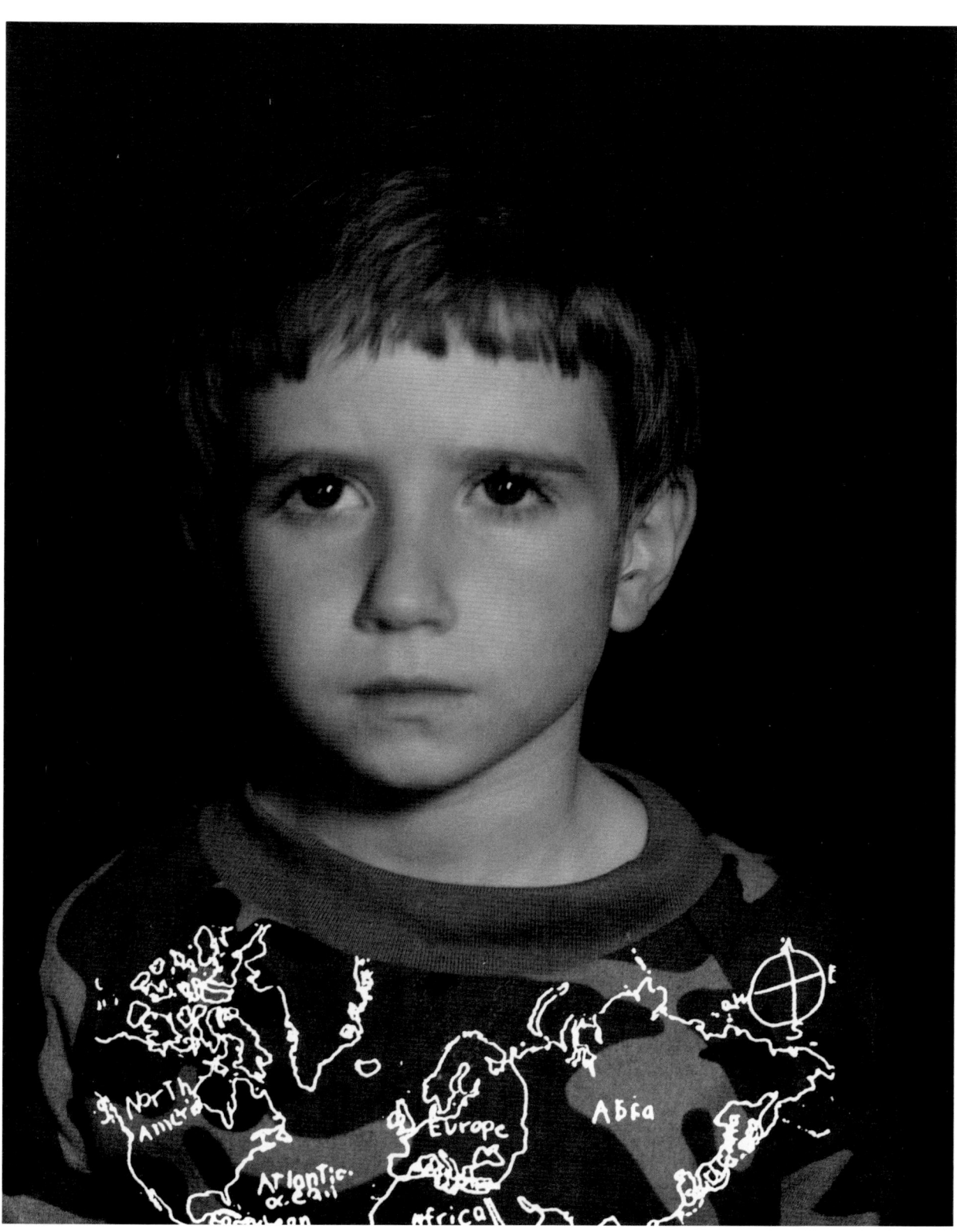

Gavin's Installation 1986

Rachel's Installation 1986

Halloween 1986: Rachel chose to be a Rainbow Bright doll and Gavin to be GI Joe.

We often talk about the power of advertisement on TV and in the stores.
The media overpowers our talk.

The picture I'm holding was taken in 1984,
the summer we moved to Illinois.
Gavin was three and Rachel six.
It was a very difficult time, a real upheaval.
Rachel really <u>was</u> sad and was very hard on her
brother who she perceived of as being happy

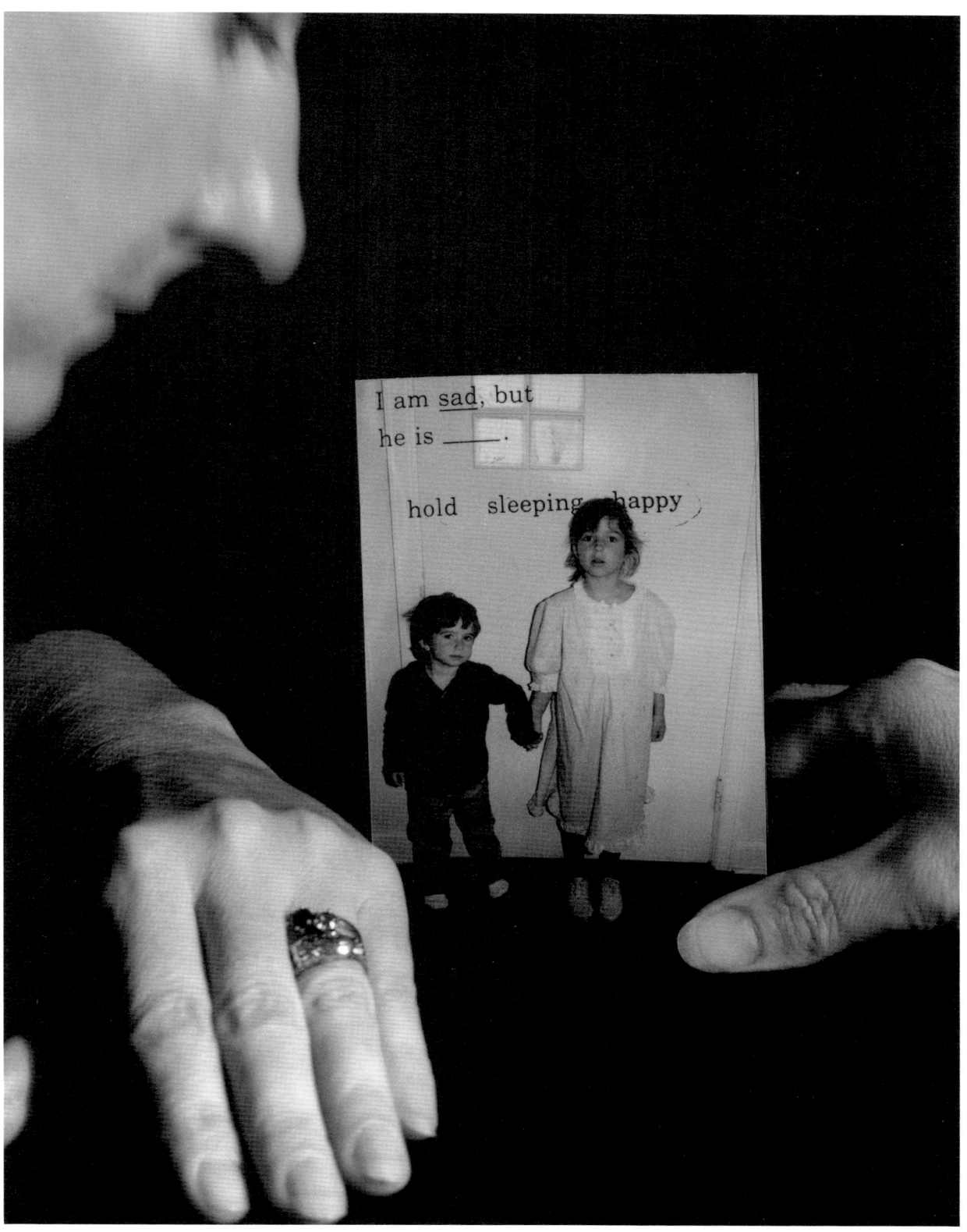

How can I teach the role of money, its worth, its relative importance?
Money buys toys...its hard to save...
there's never enough.
It is the basis of most of our weekend fights...the cause of jealousy, rage, anger, and resentment.

<u>Playing</u> with dolls is not what's fun, <u>collecting</u> them is. As soon as one doll is purchased, another with slight variations appears on the market.
Toys are sold with checklists, which work well to create an artificial need for more. Like many consumer goods, dolls have brand names.
Children know that the less expensive ones are "cheep".

feminine	masculine
princess	prince
queen	king
male	father
wife	husband
aunt	uncle
mother	female
godmother	godfather
girlfriend	boyfriend
heroine	soninlaw
daughterinlaw	hero

I will I'll
you would you'd
she will she'll
have not haven't

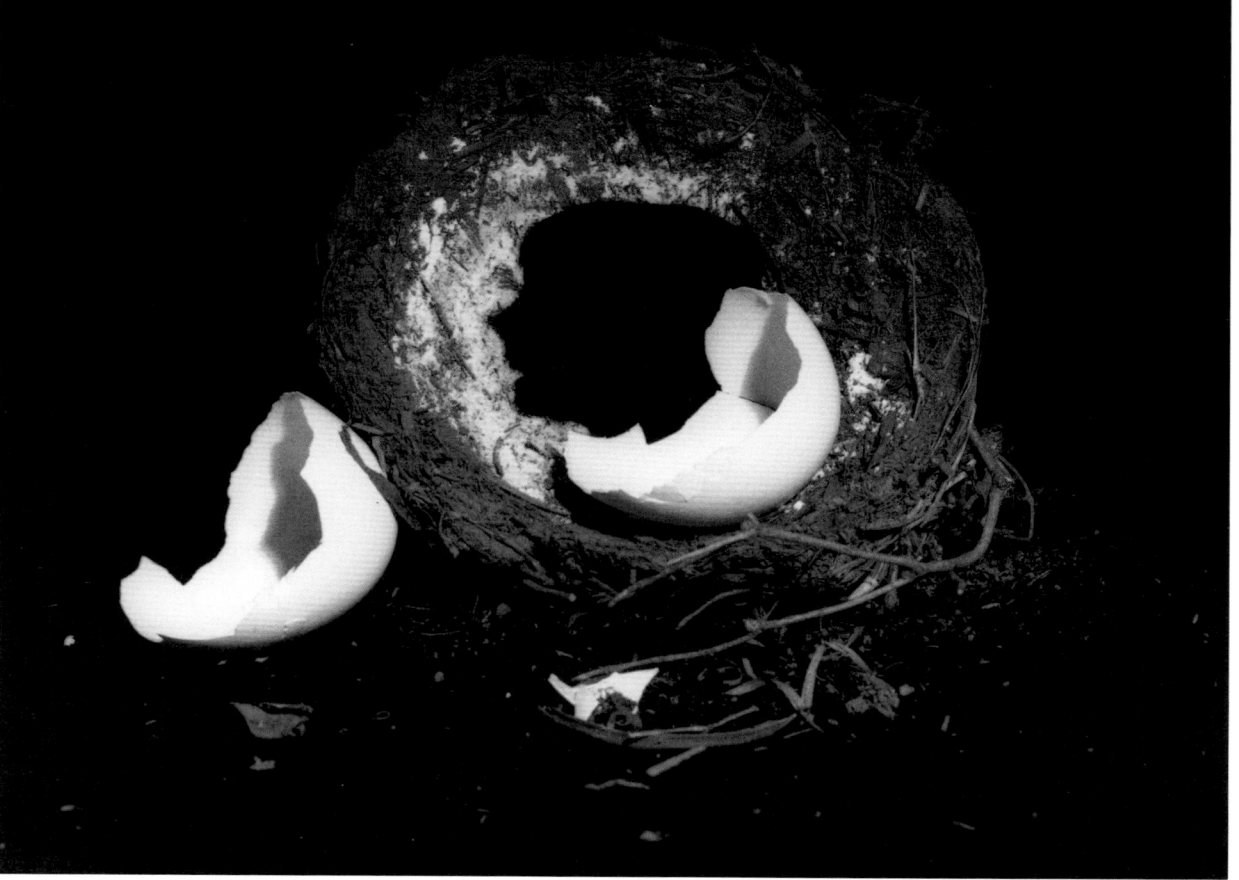

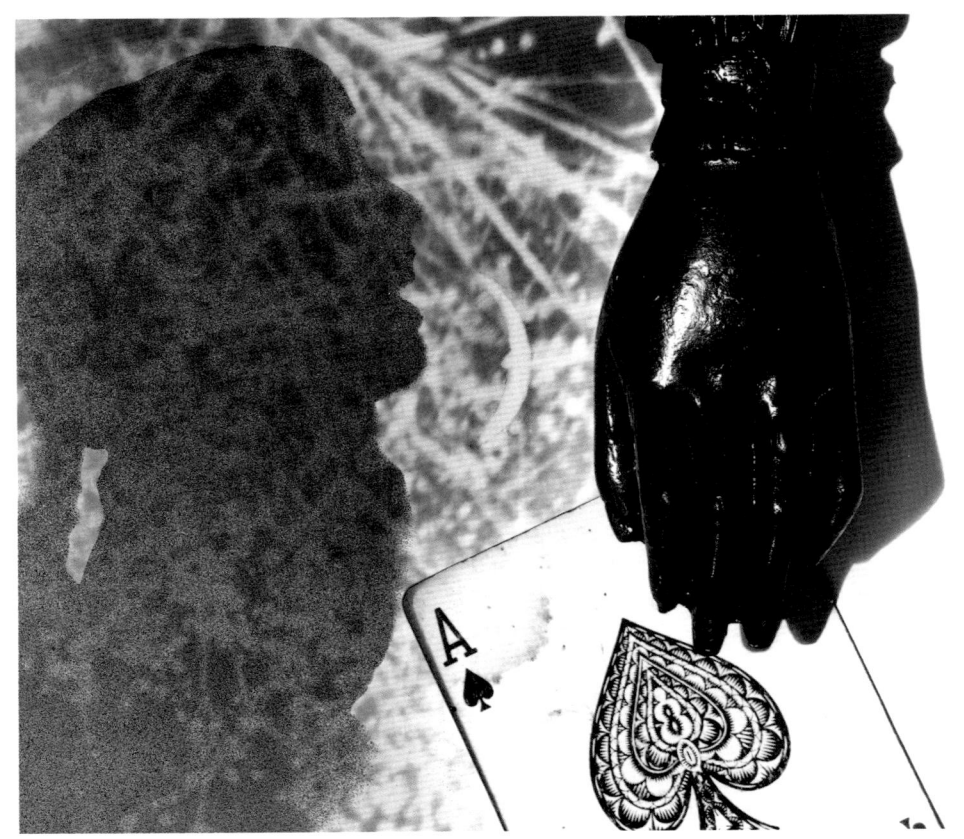

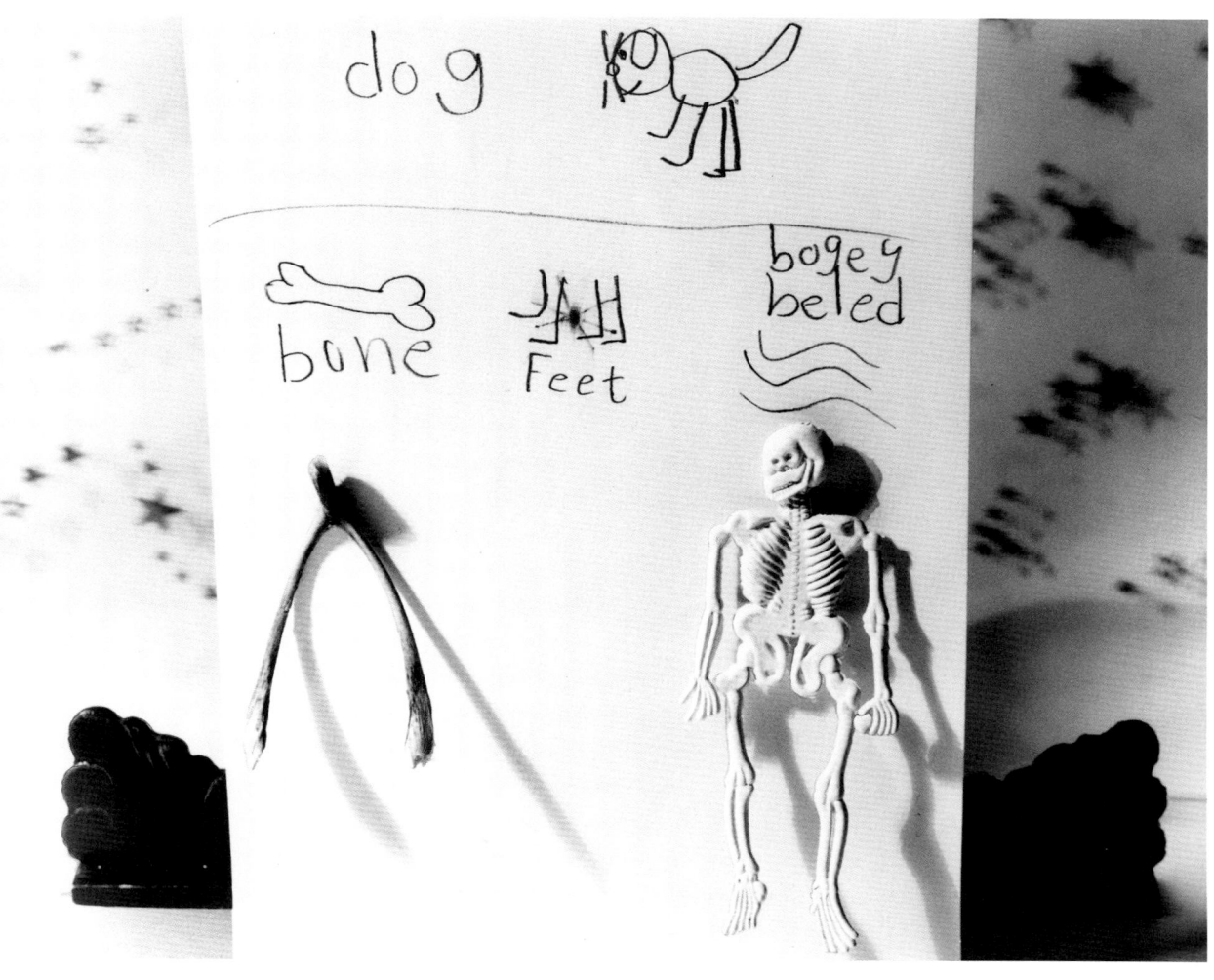

Luck is one of the most elusive lessons for my children..who can possibly explain it?

The old woman in the story of Rapunzel keeps the young one locked up... away from the world and young men. I remember the story well from my childhood. It was probably one of the reasons I grew my hair and wore it long until I turned twenty one.

The story impressed Rachel as well. She copied it word for word out of one of her books. She made a paper Rapunzel who had a yarn braid which she used to dangle out of a tower window for the Prince to ascend.

No longer the young Rapunzel,
I often feel like the witch.

Never saw the witch agen and they lived hapelie ever after.

The End

The days go by and I find raising children to be my life's most difficult undertaking. Having been raised in a family with five children, I thought I knew what it would be like to be a mother.
I was ready for some aspects of motherhood but not others.

The age old activities of separation (mother/daughter, mother/son), sibling rivalry, gender identification and character formation continue. They seem complicated in a society that values materialism, consumption, and macho aggression, while it undervalues the contributions women make.

Some days I feel powerless
while the outside forces, worries and stress
combine..compile..collect..

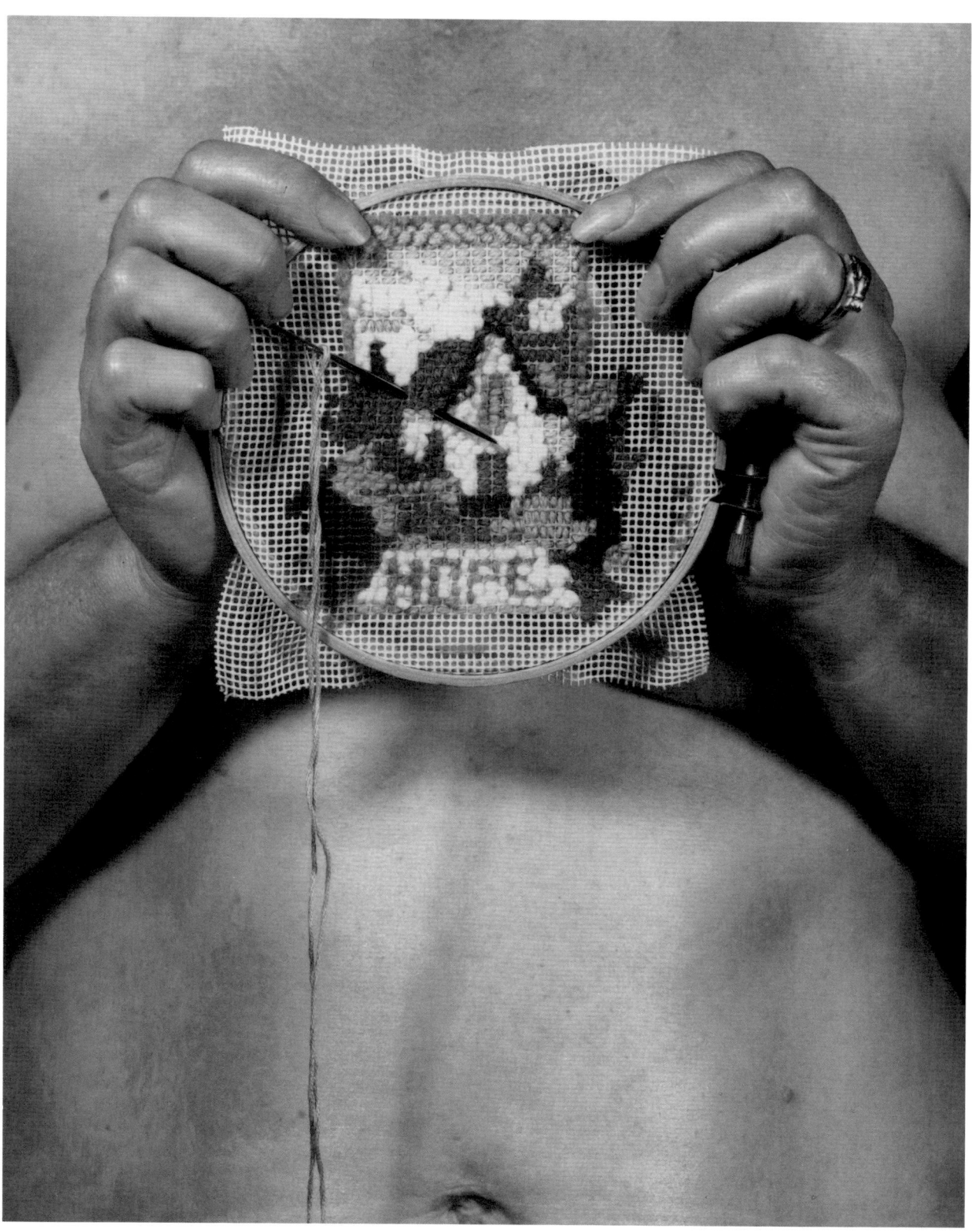

The strength and sense of honesty that I have came from my parents. Expressing my most urgent concerns through my work helps me to cope with the demands placed upon me. It is my hope that my strength will pass on to my children, helping them to learn life's lessons and survive unbroken and able to contribute something positive to this world.